One Million and One
The OUR WORLD Series

1,000,001
Amazing Pets

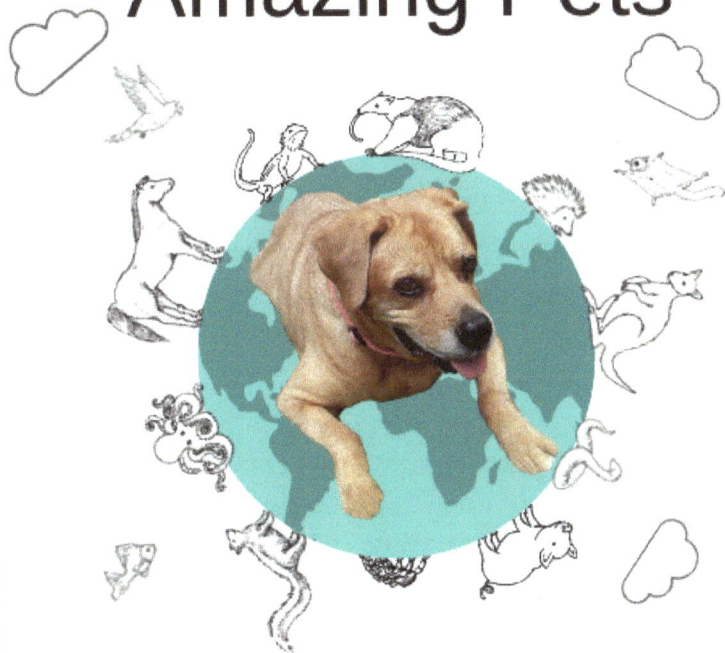

Connie Goyette Crawley

Dedicated to Dr. Kelly Alford,
an extraordinary vet
and an even more extraordinary person.
Your generosity brightened our world.

Book 2 of
One Million and One: The OUR WORLD Series

Published by 3DLight Publications
Fayetteville, GA
Text copyright © 2018
Connie Goyette Crawley
conniecrawley.com

ISBN: 978-0-9986614-7-6
1st Edition

3DLight
Publications

All over the world, people share their lives with animals. Although not all animals are suited to be pets, with over 20,000,000,000,000,000,000 (20 QUINTILLION!) animals on earth, there are at least a million choices of amazing pets!

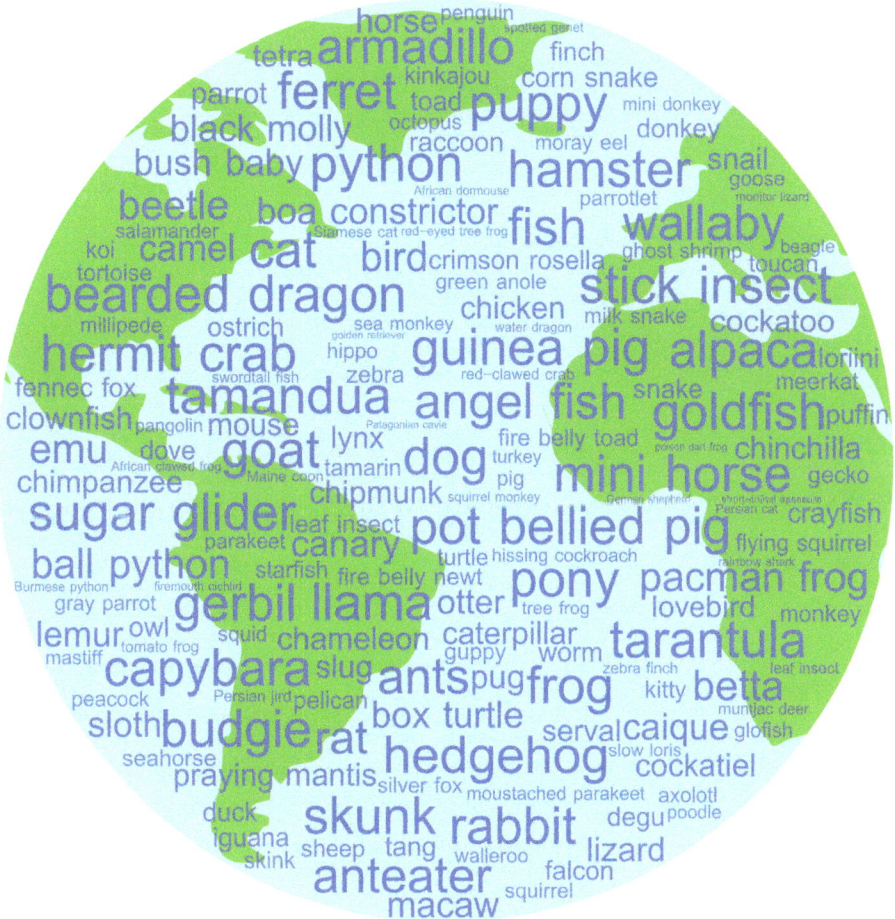

$$\begin{array}{r} 1,000,000 \text{ pets} \\ + \text{ YOUR perfect pet} \\ \hline 1,000,001 \text{ pets} \end{array}$$

amazing

1. See pictures of some of the world's most amazing pets.

2. Read interesting facts about unusual pets.

Llama

Llamas are closely related to camels. They are friendly, curious, and easy to train. Llamas don't bite, but spit clear saliva or a disgusting green goo when annoyed or frightened. Mama llamas hum to their babies - and the babies hum back.

CANADA

UNITED STATES

MEXICO

CUBA

VENEZUELA

COLOMBIA

ECUADOR

PERU

BOLIVIA

PARAGUAY

BRAZ

CHILE

ARGENTINA   URUGUA

Legend

☐ Water

🟧 Emu range

4. Use the map legend to see where the animals live in the wild.

3.

Scientific Name

common octopus

Octopus vulgaris

/ **ok**-tuh-pus   vul-**gar**-us /

Learn the scientific names of animals.

Scientific names are Latin or Greek words that scientists use to describe plants and animals.
Use the phonetic spelling to sound out the syllables.
Give the most emphasis to the syllables in bold.

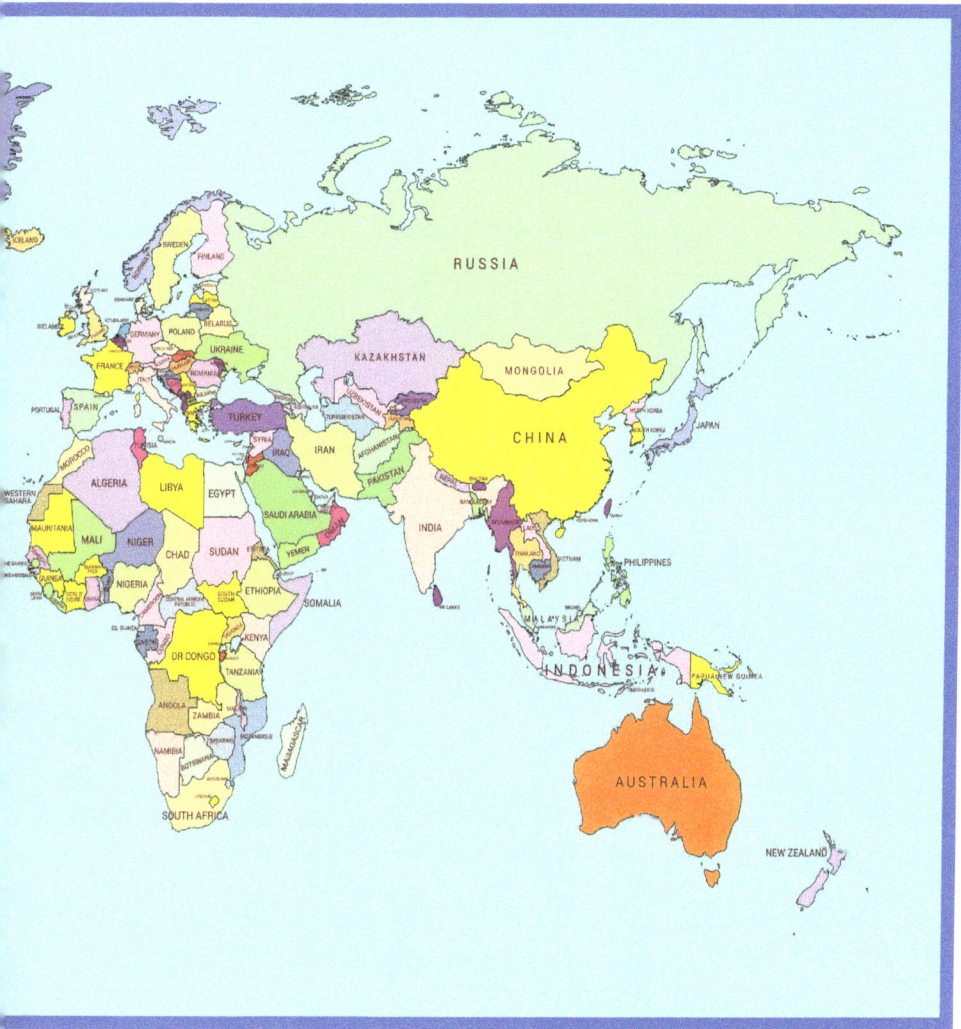

5.

Group
Name:

a prickle of
hedgehogs

**Learn the
funny names for
groups of animals.**

6.

Read ten top tips for choosing a pet.

Top Tips for Choosing a Pet

1. Is the pet available for adoption from a shelter? There's a rescue or adoption organization for just about every type of pet.
2. Can you give the pet the attention and care that it will need?

European hedgehog

Erinaceus europaeus

\ er-ih-**nay**-shuhs   yoor-uh-**pee**-uhs \

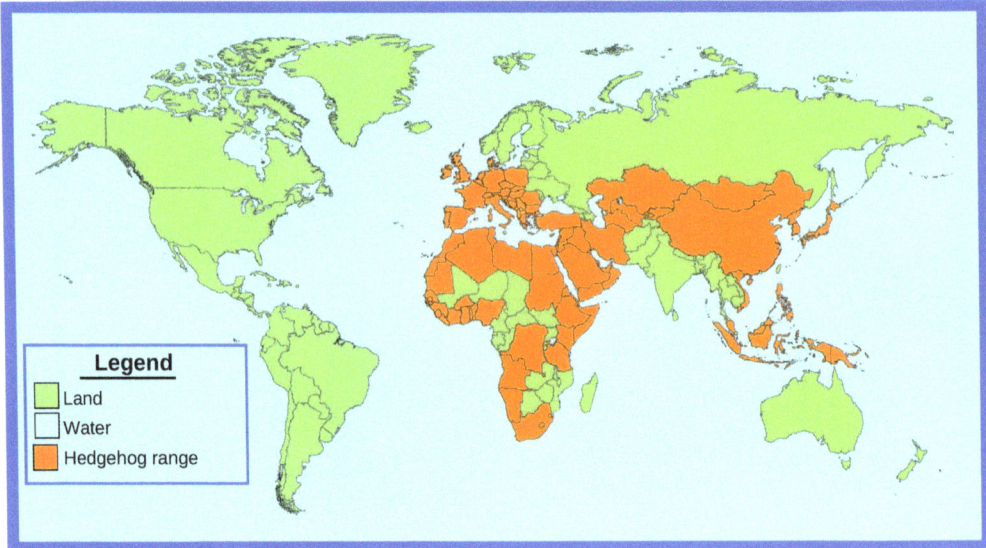

Legend
- Land
- Water
- Hedgehog range

- There are several species of hedgehogs, including the European hedgehog, the African pygmy hedgehog, and the long-earred hedgehog.

- Hedgehogs got their name from the way they make their homes in hedges and bushes and because they sometimes make a grunting sound like a pig.

- They eat frogs, earthworms, beetles, ants, grasshoppers, and other insects.

- Baby hedgehogs are called hoglets or pups.

- Hedgehogs are nocturnal and have very poor eyesight.

Hedgehog

A hedgehog has about 5,000 spines. Each spine is actually a hollow, stiff hair. When hedgehogs roll into a ball, their spines stick out. Spines last about a year, then fall out and are replaced- just like the hair of a dog, cat, or human. It is illegal to own a hedgehog in some US states and some parts of Canada.

Group name:

a prickle of hedgehogs

common octopus

Octopus vulgaris

/ **ok**-tuh-pus   vul-**gar**-uhs /

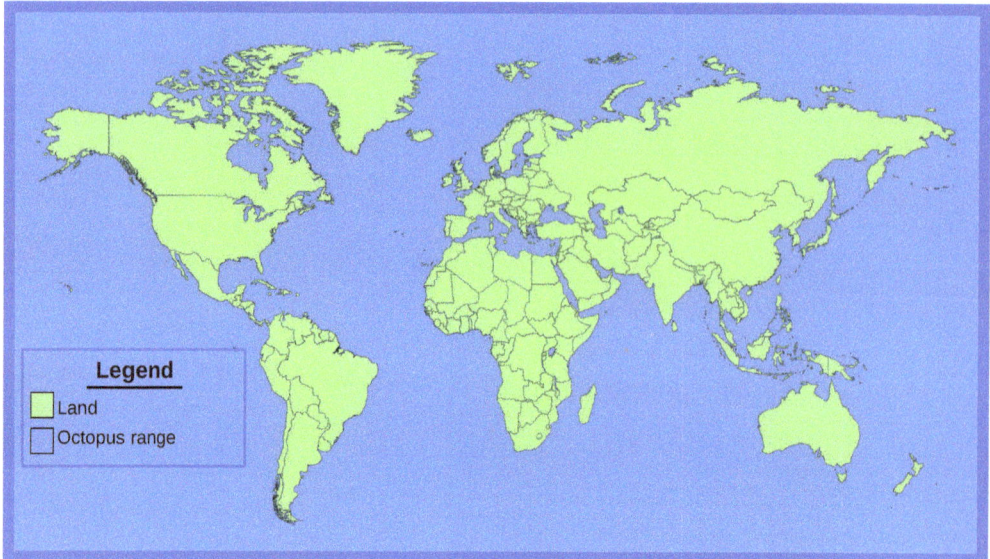

Legend

- Land
- Octopus range

- Octopuses can be found in every ocean in the world. They often live in coral reefs and rock crevices.

- An octopus has 3 hearts. Its blood is blue.

- If an enemy attacks, an octopus can break off its arm to escape. Then the octopus can regrow the arm.

- An octopus propels itself through the water by sucking in water and then blasting it out through a tube-like siphon.

- The largest recorded octopus had an arm span of over 30 feet.

- Octopuses do not have bones so their bodies are very flexible. They can squeeze into small spaces.

Daiju Azuma / CC BY-SA 2.5 Wikimedia Commons

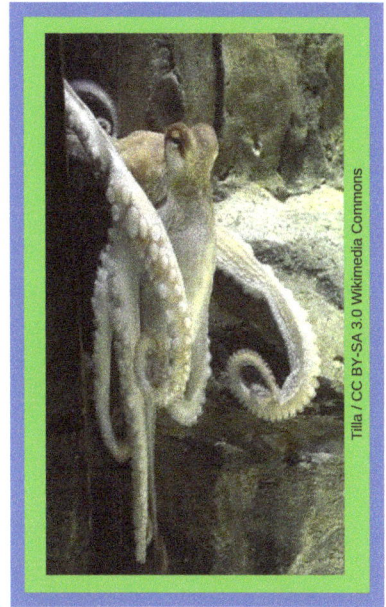

Tilla / CC BY-SA 3.0 Wikimedia Commons

Octopus

Octopuses are very smart - smart enough to escape from their tanks! They have eight arms with up to 240 suction cups on each arm. An octopus can change color to blend in with its surroundings. It can confuse predators by squirting a cloud of black ink.

Group name:

a consortium of octopuses

Boris Mrdja / shutterstock.com

Legend
- Land
- Water
- Capybara range

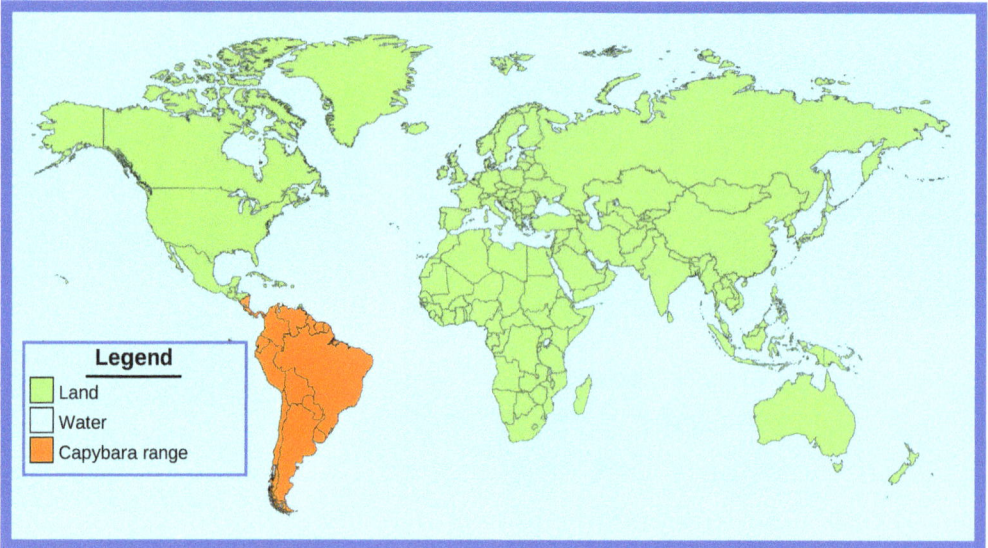

- Capybaras are native to Central and South America. They're most common in Panama, Colombia, Peru, Venezuela, and Brazil.

- They live in forests and savannas, near bodies of water. They eat water plants and grasses.

- Capybaras have webbed toes like a duck.

- Mother capybaras give birth to 4-5 babies at a time. The babies are called pups.

- When they sense danger, capybaras make a barking sound. They also purr, whistle, squeal, and grunt.

<u>Capybara</u>

Capybaras are the world's largest rodent. They are closely related to guinea pigs and grow to be about four feet long with a weight of over 140 pounds. In the wild, capybaras live in large groups. They are good swimmers and can stay under water for up to 5 minutes.

Group name:

a herd of capybaras

Scientific Name	**sugar glider**
	Petaurus breviceps
	/ **pet**-or-uhs **brev**-ih-seps /

Legend
- Land
- Water
- Sugar glider range

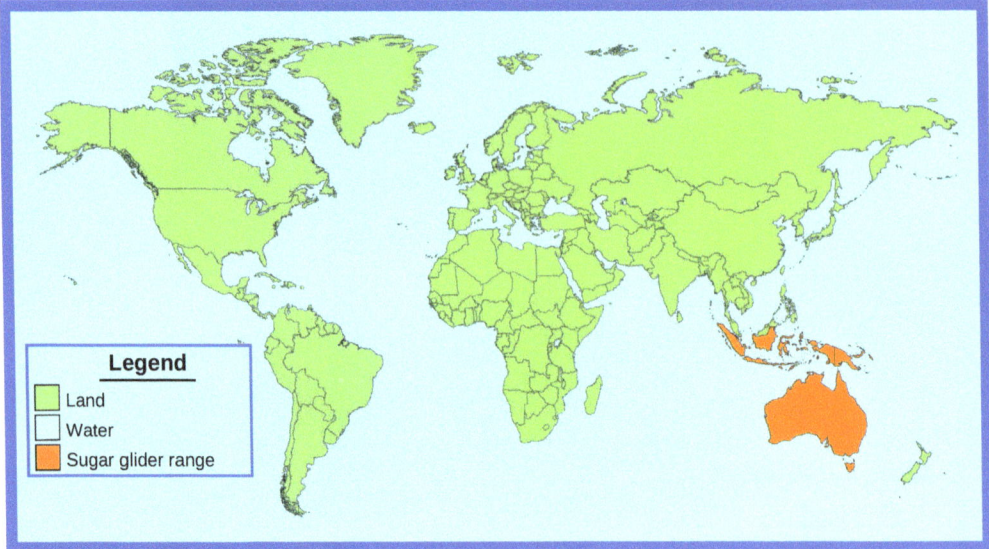

- Sugar gliders live in the tree tops in Australia, Indonesia, and New Guinea. They are nocturnal.

- Sugar gliders look like small squirrels but are marsupials, like kangaroos.

- Like other marsupials, baby sugar gliders are called joeys. After birth, a joey crawls into the mother's pouch where it will be warm and safe. Later, it will come out to explore.

- An adult sugar glider is about 12-13 inches long - from the tip of its nose to the tip of its tail.

- A sugar glider's tail is long and flat and helps it to balance and steer while gliding. The tail is prehensile, which means it can be used to hold onto leaves and twigs.

Sugar Glider

Sugar gliders get their name from their love of sugary fruits and from the way they glide from tree to tree. A stretchy flap of skin, called a patagium, connects their front and back legs. When a sugar glider jumps, it spreads its legs and glides through the air. Sugar gliders can glide over 164 feet.

Group name:

a colony of sugar gliders

miniature horse

Equus ferus caballus

\ **ek**-wus **fair**-us **cab**-uh-luhs \

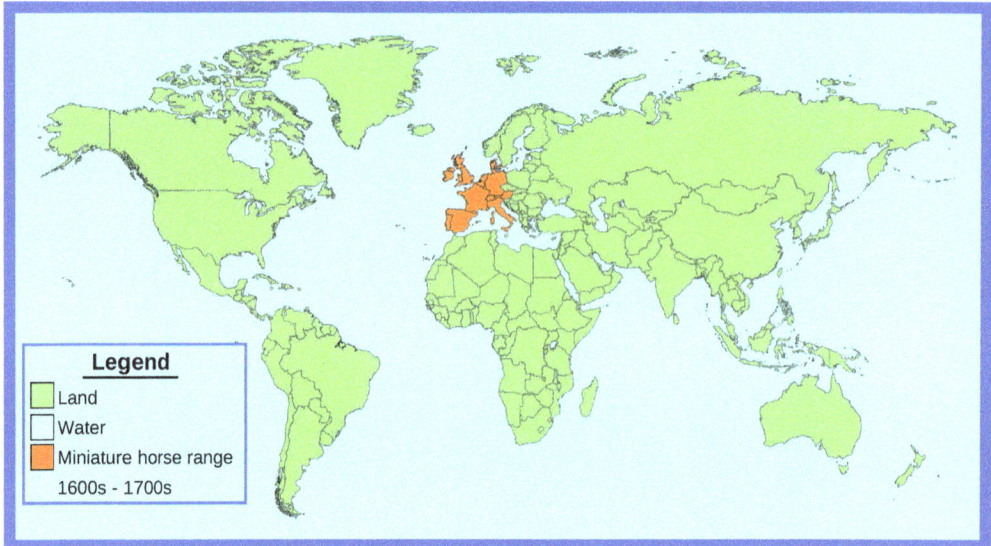

Legend
- Land
- Water
- Miniature horse range 1600s - 1700s

- Miniature horses were first bred in Europe in the 1600's as pets for royalty.

- They were brought to the United States to work in coal mines because their small size allowed them to work in underground tunnels.

- A small horse is often referred to as a pony but miniature horses are different from ponies because:

  - a pony is a type of small horse but with shorter, thicker legs and a thicker coat.

  - miniature horses have been bred to look just like a tiny version of a horse, with a slender neck and long, thin legs.

Miniature Horse

Miniature horses are bred for their small size. Most are 34 to 38 inches tall, from the ground to the base of their neck. Mini horses tend to be friendly and gentle. Some have been trained to help people with disabilities or to visit hospitals with their handlers.

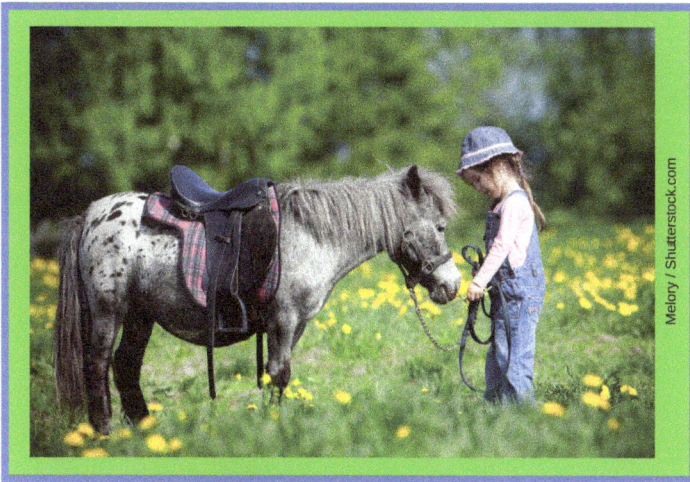

Melory / Shutterstock.com

Group name:

a string of miniature horses

38 inches

central bearded dragon
Pogono vitticeps
/ puh-**go**-nuh **vit**-ee-seps /

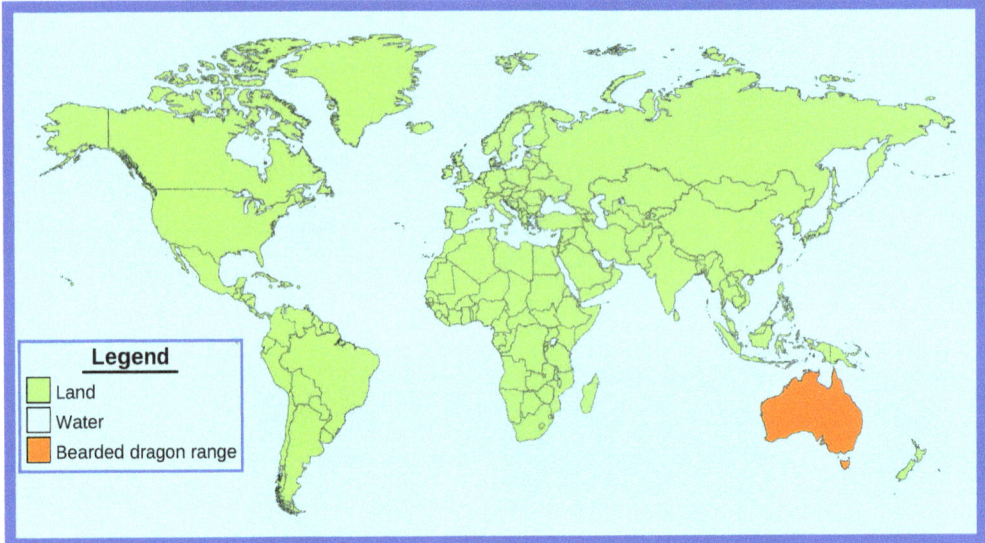

Legend
- Land
- Water
- Bearded dragon range

- Bearded dragons are found throughout Australia, in both desert regions and woodlands.

- They will eat just about anything including plants, insects, small rodents, and other lizards.

- Beardies can grow to be up to 24 inches long. Their tail makes up at least half of their length.

- Bearded dragons produce a mild venom which is usually harmless to humans.

- Beardies can be green, red, orange or yellow - depending on the color of the soil in their natural environment. They can change the color of their backs to a darker shade to absorb more of the sun's energy.

Bearded Dragon

Bearded dragons, or "beardies", are a type of lizard. When a beardie puffs out its throat, its spiny scales stand up, and looks like a beard. Beardies sometimes wave their front legs as a sign of submission. It looks as if they're saying hello.

Group name:

a lounge of lizards

northern tamandua

Tamandua mexicana

/ tuh-**man**-doo-wuh   mex-ee-**con**-uh /

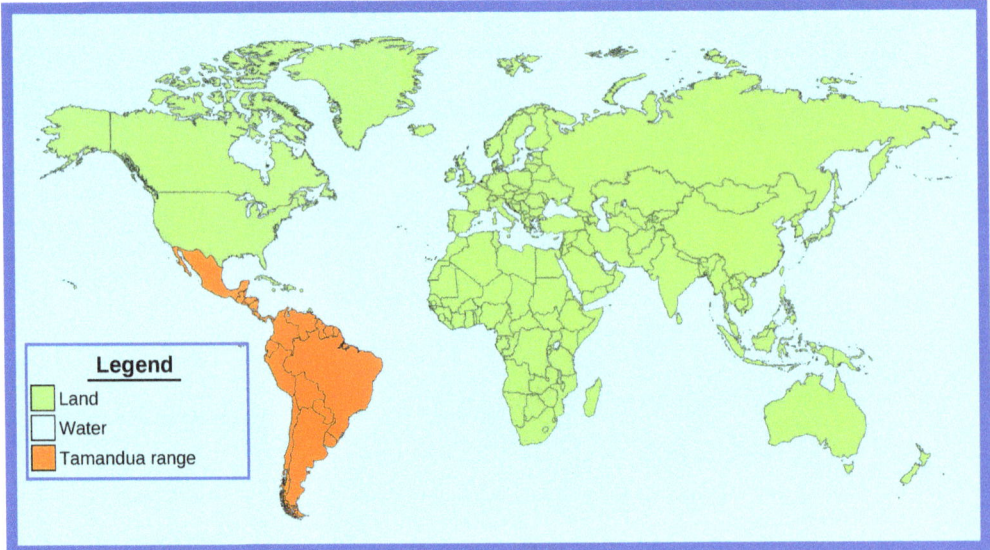

Legend
- Land
- Water
- Tamandua range

- Tamanduas can be found in the forests and grasslands of Central and South America and in Mexico.

- They are also known as "lesser anteaters" because they are much smaller than their relatives, the giant anteater. They are sometimes called "ant bears".

- Tamanduas can hold onto things with their prehensile tail which is like the tail of monkeys and seahorses. They use it to hold on while climbing trees and for balance when they stand. They also use their tail as a pillow.

- Like skunks, tamanduas protect themselves by releasing a stinky smell. They are sometimes called the stinkers of the forest.

<u>Tamandua</u>

Tamanduas are a type of anteater. They do not have teeth but use their long snouts and sticky tongues to eat about 9,000 ants a day. They also eat termites, bees, and honey. Tamanduas spend most of their time in trees. They move awkwardly on the ground.

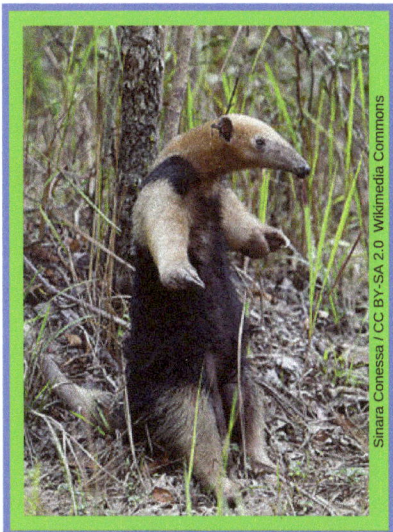

Group name:

A group of any sort of anteater is called a candle of anteaters.

17

Scientific Name	ball python
	Python regius
	/ **py**-thon ruh-**jee**-uhs /

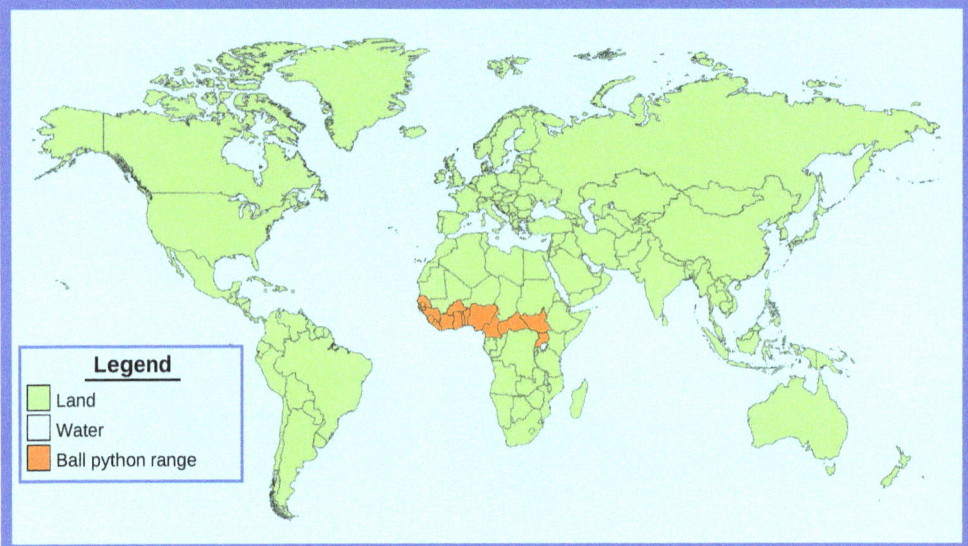

Legend
- Land
- Water
- Ball python range

- Ball pythons are found in west and central Africa.

- They are also known as Royal Pythons because of stories that African royalty used to wear them wrapped around their arms as jewelry.

- Female pythons are typically larger than males.

- Pythons are constrictors. They coil around their prey and squeeze to kill it.

- Ball pythons can live to be about 30 years old. A ball python at the Philadelphia Zoo lived to be 47 years old.

Sipa / Pixabay.com CC0 - public domain

Ball Python

The ball python got its name because, when it senses danger, it curls into a ball, with its head tucked into the middle. Like other snakes, it has a sensitive forked tongue. Ball pythons grow to be about 3-5 feet long and are not venomous.

Group name:

a nest of pythons

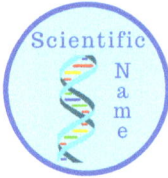

Legend
- Land
- Water
- Llama range

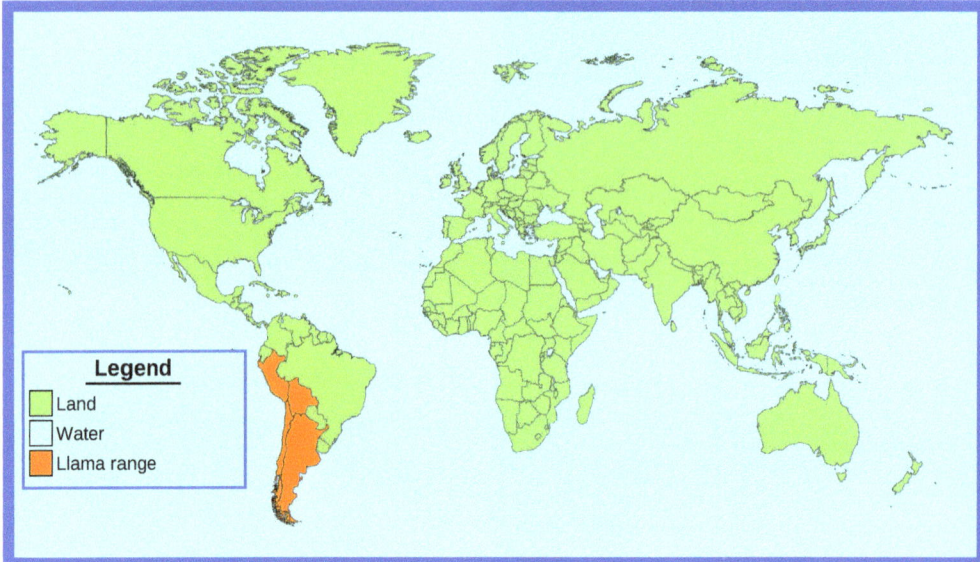

- Llamas live in the Andes mountains. They are most common in Peru, Argentina, Bolivia and Chile.

- Llamas were domesticated by the Incas about 6,000 years ago.

- They can live for up to 30 years. They grow to be over six feet tall and can weigh over 400 pounds.

- They are herbivores and eat many types of grasses.

- Like camels, llamas have soft pads on the bottom of their feet. They have two big toenails on each foot.

- Llamas are covered in wool. Llama wool is used to make sweaters, blankets, hats, and scarves.

Llama

Llamas are closely related to camels. They are friendly, curious, and easy to train. Llamas don't bite, but can spit clear saliva or a disgusting green goo when annoyed or frightened. Mama llamas hum to their babies - and the babies hum back.

Group name:

a flock of llamas

Legend
Land
Water
Emu range

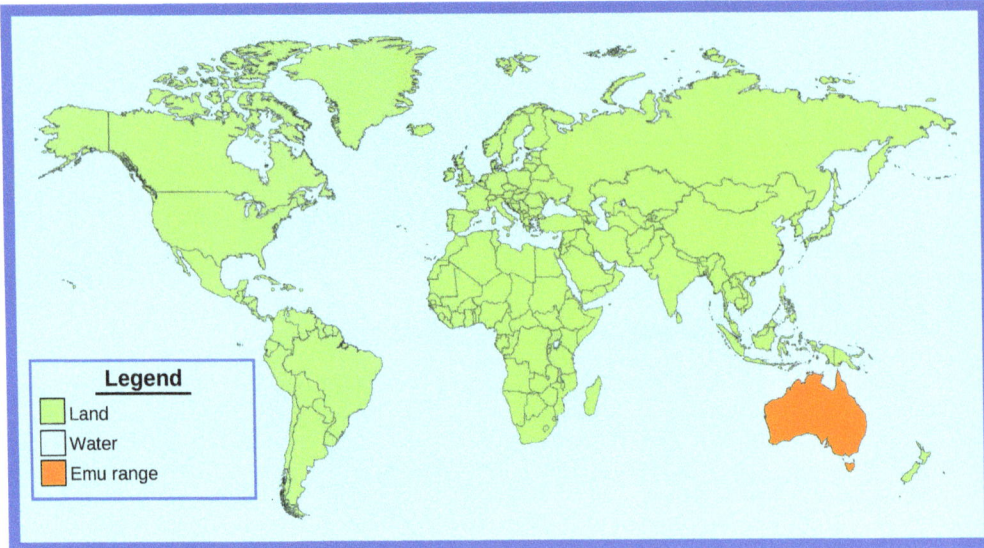

- Emus are native to Australia, where they live in open country. Their relative, the ostrich, is native to Africa.

- Emus can grow to be over six feet tall.

- They eat many kinds of plants and insects, but can go for weeks without food.

- Female emus lay greenish-blue eggs. Male emus protects the eggs and watch over the chicks after they hatch.

- Emus protect themselves by running in a zig-zag pattern, jumping, and kicking.

CC0 1.0 - Max Pixel / Public Domain

Emu

Emus are the second largest bird in the world – right after their cousin, the ostrich. Emus can't fly but are fast runners, and can reach speeds of over 30 miles per hour. Emus can be aggressive and have sharp claws on their 3-toed feet. They can deliver a powerful kick!

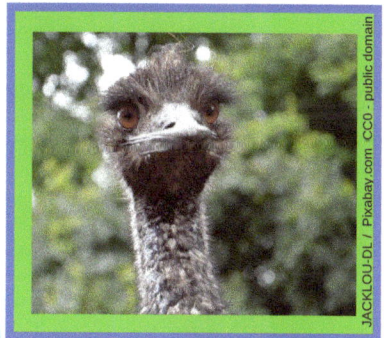

JACKLOU-DL / Pixabay.com -CC0 - public domain

Group name:

a mob of emus

striped skunk

Mephitis mephitis

/ **mef**-it-is   **mef**-it-is /

Legend

Land
Water
Skunk range

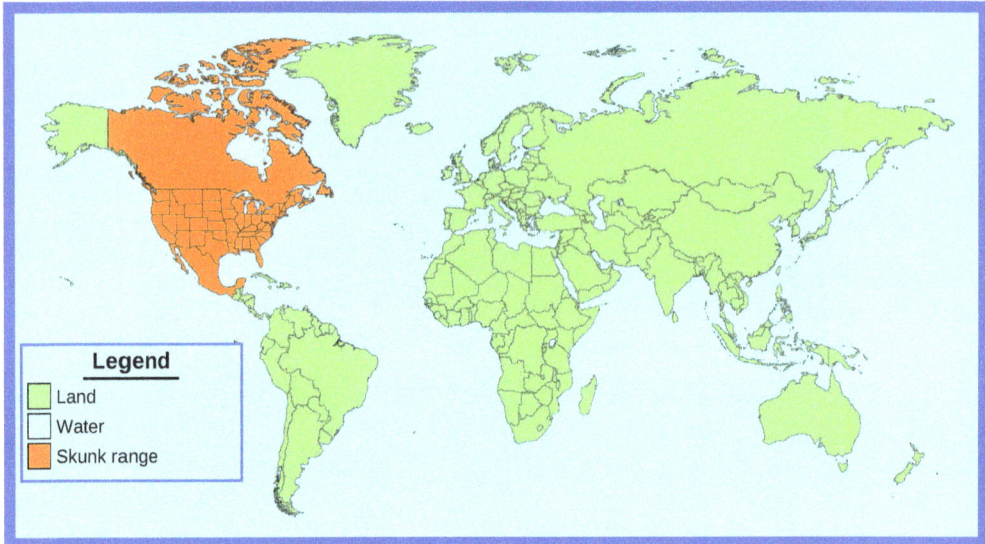

- Skunks are native to North America. However, it's illegal to have a pet skunk in most U.S. states.

- In the wild, skunks eat plants and small animals like worms, frogs, snakes, and birds.

- Skunks are very intelligent and are great problem-solvers. They can learn to open cabinets, drawers, and even refrigerators. They love to pull blankets from a bed to make a nest for themselves.

- Skunks require a lot of attention and are generally not good pets to have around young children. People who have pet skunks say that a skunk will never forget someone who pulls its tail.

birdphotos.com / CC BY 3.0 via Wikimedia Commons

Skunk

In the wild, skunks hiss, stomp their feet, and puff up as a warning before lifting their tail to spray their bad-smelling scent. After spraying, it takes a skunk about a week to restock its spray supply. Most pet skunks have had their scent glands removed.

Group name:

a surfeit of skunks

CC0 – public domain / GFLD

Phryganistria chinensis Zhao
(world's largest stick insect)
/ fry-gan-**eest**-ree-uh   **kin**-en-sis   **jow** /

Legend

Land
Water
Stick insect range

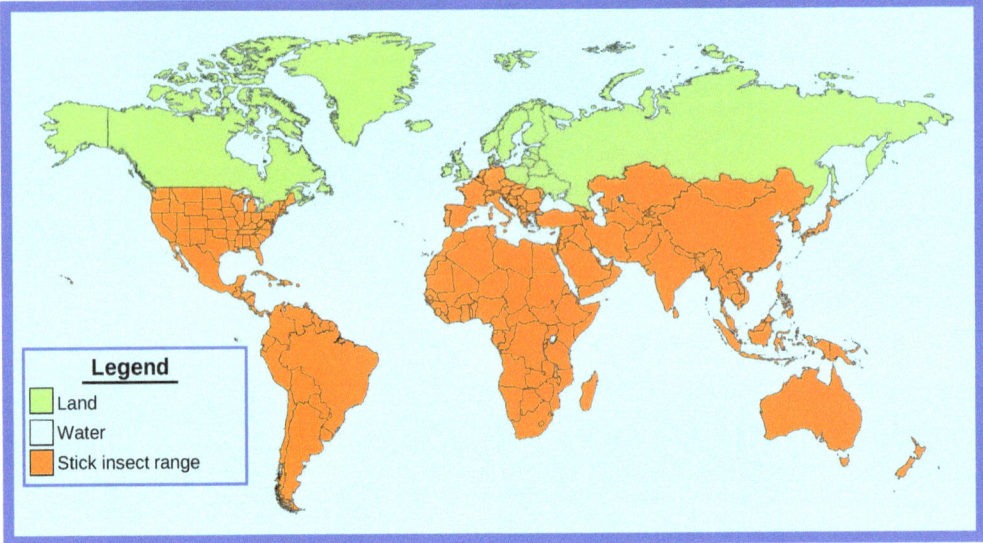

- Stick insects can be found on every continent except for Antarctica. They are most common in tropical areas.

- There are over 6000 species of stick insects.

- Like any insect, a stick insect has 6 legs and 2 antennae.

- Stick insects can trick predators by swaying in the breeze so they look like part of a tree or bush.

- If a stick insect loses a leg, it can grow another one.

- The largest stick insect ever discovered was found in southern China. The *Phryganistria chinensis Zhao* is almost 25 inches long.

Stick Insect

Stick insects are the world's longest insect. Some types are over 13 inches long. Stick insects are related to grasshoppers and praying mantises. Also called stick bugs or walking sticks, they are easy to care for and are a popular insect pet.

Group name:

a bushel of stick insects

Scientific Name	**red-necked wallaby**
	Macropus rufogriseus
	/ ma-**crow**-puhs **roo**-fuh-**gree**-see-uhs /

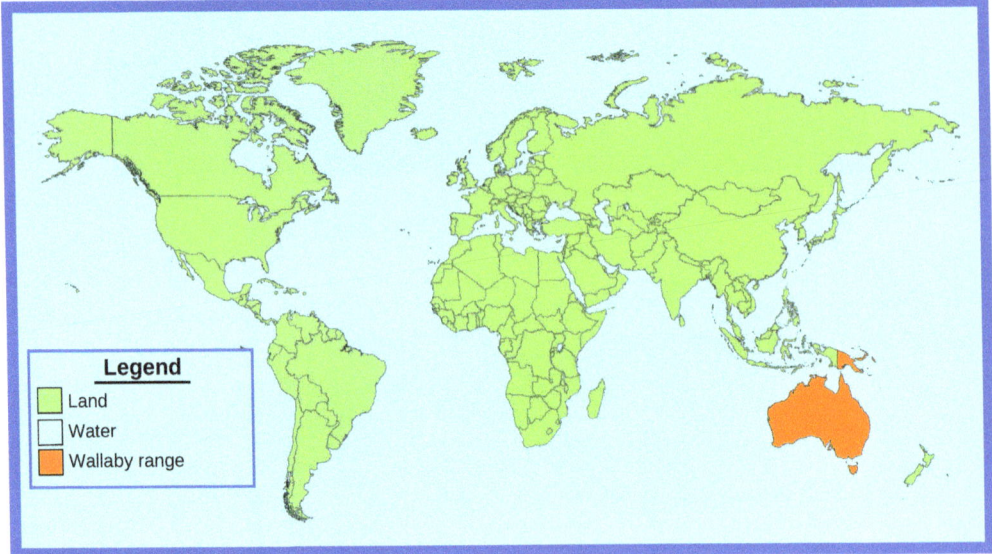

- Wallabies are similar to kangaroos but are smaller. They are native to Australia and New Guinea.

- They use their strong hind legs for hopping, to balance when they sit, and to kick predators.

- Their long, powerful tails helps to push them forward as they hop.

- Large wallabies can hop at speeds of 30 miles an hour.

- Wallabies thump the ground with their feet to warn other wallabies of danger.

- Like other marsupials, only the female has a pouch.

Wallaby

Like kangaroos, wallabies are marsupials. Marsupial babies are tiny and pink at birth and crawl into the mother's pouch to stay for several months. Then the babies come out to explore but crawl back inside if danger is near. Young wallabies are called "joeys".

Group name:

a mob of wallabies

domestic pig

Sus scrofa domesticus

/ **soos** **skro**-fuh duh-mes-**tik**-uhs /

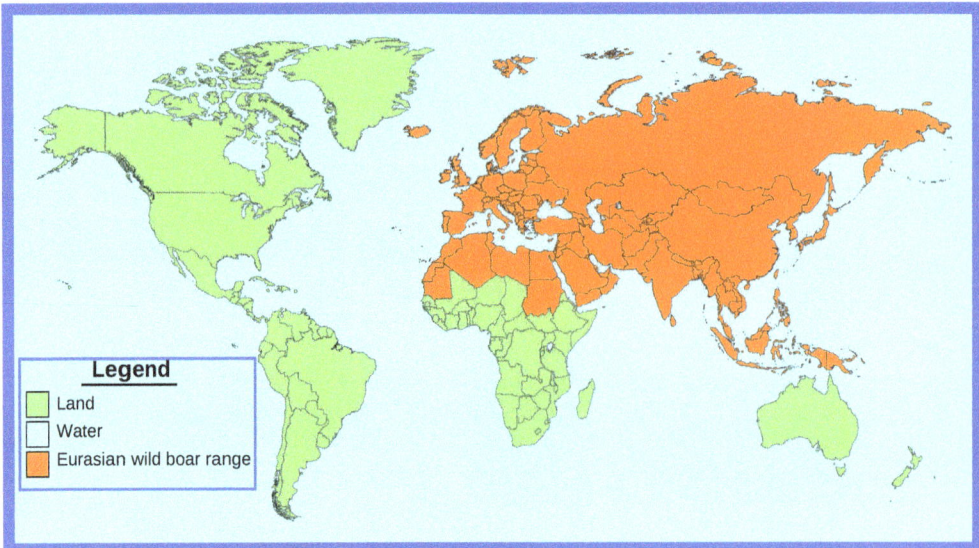

Legend
Land
Water
Eurasian wild boar range

- Domestic pigs are related to the wild boars of Europe, Asia, and North Africa. They were first domesticated in China about 9,000 years ago.

- Miniature pigs are bred from several different types of domestic pigs. There are at least 14 different miniature pig breeds.

- Pigs are very intelligent and social animals. They learn quickly and have good memories. They can be trained to walk on a leash, use a litter box, and do tricks.

- Pigs have poor eyesight but an excellent sense of smell. They have been trained to sniff out truffles, drugs, and explosives.

Miniature Pig

Mini pigs, teacup pigs,
micro pigs, pot-bellied pigs,
pocket pigs, and Juliana pigs
have all been bred to be smaller
than a typical farm pig.
Some people buy miniature pigs as
babies, thinking that they will
remain small. But miniature pigs
can grow to weigh over
100 pounds.

Group name:

a drift
of pigs

Scientific Name

Grammostola rosea

/ **gram**-muh-sto-luh **rose**-ay-uh /

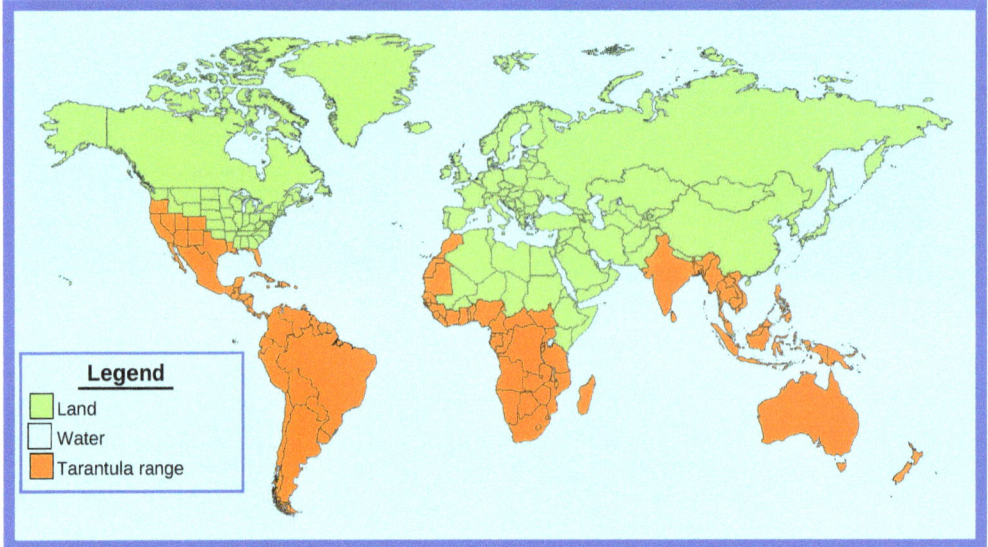

Legend
- Land
- Water
- Tarantula range

- There are about 900 species of tarantulas. Most are found in South America, but tarantulas can also be found in North America, Africa, Asia, and Australia.

- Tarantulas are nocturnal hunters. Large tarantulas eat lizards, snakes, bats, frogs, and rodents.

- Some species live in the ground. Others live in trees.

- A common type of pet tarantula is the Chilean rose tarantula. It is also called the Chilean fire tarantula.

- Tarantulas that live in the ground have chunky bodies. Tree tarantulas are sleek with longer legs.

- If a tarantula loses a leg, it can grow a new one.

Tarantula

Tarantulas are the largest spiders in the world. They are quiet pets and need very little space but can be injured easily when handled. Tarantulas are venomous but for most people, a tarantula's bite is no more dangerous than a bee sting.

Group name:

A group of any sort of spider is called a clutter of spiders.

Missie26870 / pixabay.com CC0 - public domain

Legend
- Land
- Water
- Budgerigar range

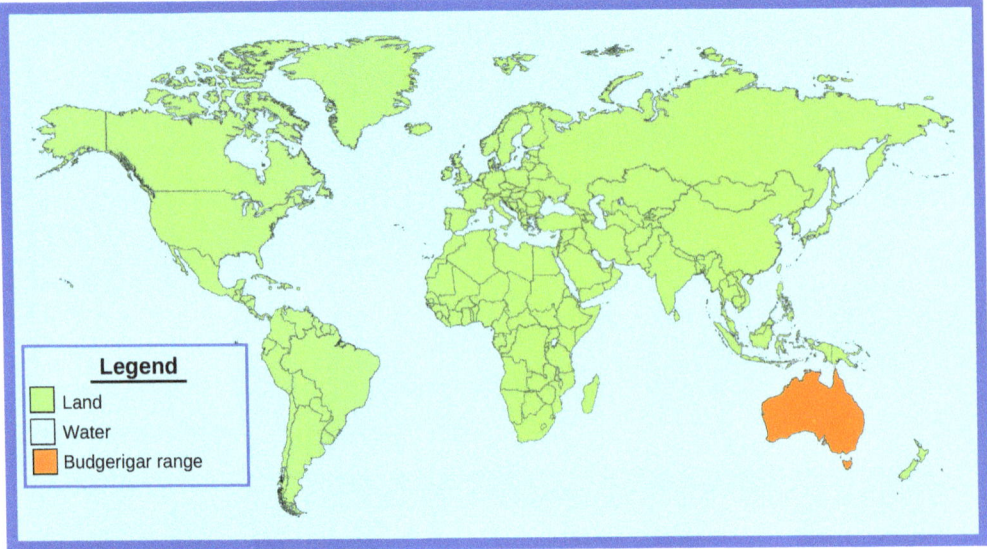

- A budgie is a type of Australian parakeet, or small parrot, and is the most popular type of pet bird in the world.

- In the wild, budgies are green. Pet budgies are bred to be blue, white, yellow, violet, and gray.

- They have two toes that face forward on each foot and two toes that face backward.

- Budgies have a small bump called a *cere* above their beak. Males have a blue cere. A female's cere is brown, beige or white.

- Budgies are flock birds and are happiest living with other budgies.

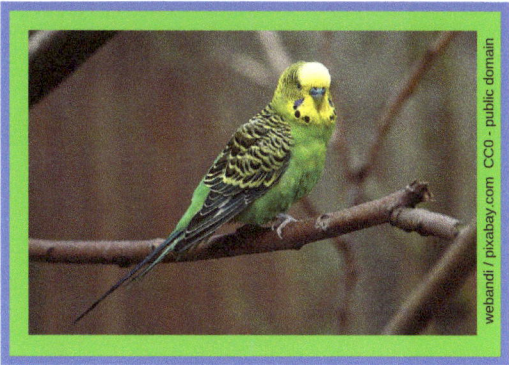

webandi / pixabay.com CC0 - public domain

Budgie

A budgie, or budgerigar, is a type of small parrot. Budgies can learn to imitate words and phrases. Puck, a male budgie, was listed in the *Guinness Book of World Records* as having the largest vocabulary of any bird in the world. Puck could say over 1,728 words and phrases!

Group name:

a chatter of budgies

Der Knipser / pixabay.com CC0 - public domain

Argentine horned frog

Ceratophrys ornata

/ **seer**-uh-taw-fris   or-**not**-uh /

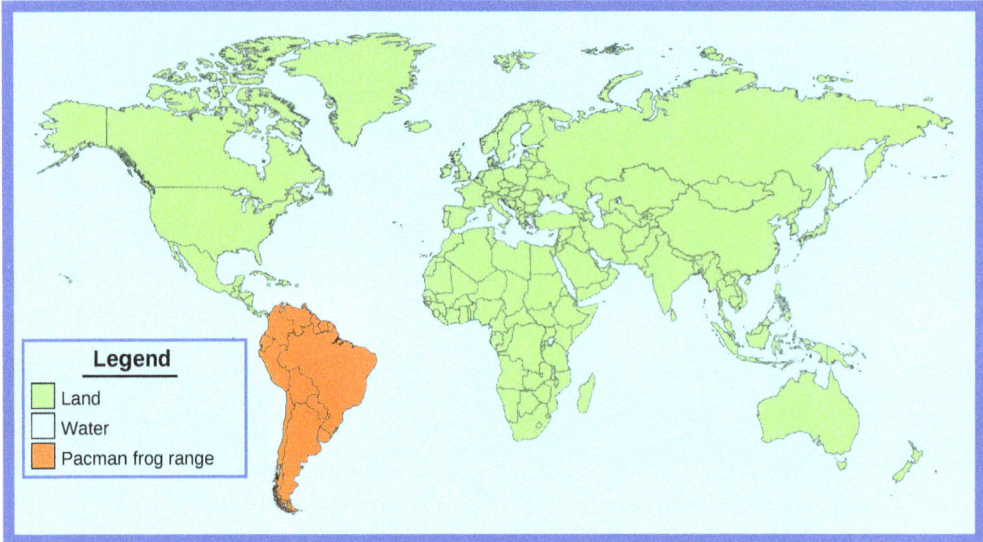

Legend
- Land
- Water
- Pacman frog range

- The Pacman frog is one of several types of South American horned frogs. They are also known as Argentine wide-mouthed frogs.

- These tropical frogs are found on the moist forest floors of Argentina, Paraguay, Uruguay, and Brazil.

- Pacman frogs grow to be up to 7 inches long.

- They will eat anything that they can fit into their mouths: insects, fish, worms, reptiles, mice, and even other horned frogs.

- Pacman frogs burrow into a hole with just their eyes showing. They wait for food to come by and then jump out and gobble it up.

Pacman Frog

Pacman frogs are like a giant mouth with legs attached. They are aggressive and attack predators (or humans) with their tiny, sharp teeth. Like other amphibians, Pacman frogs have sensitive skin and should be handled as little as possible.

Group name:

an army of frogs

Popular Pets

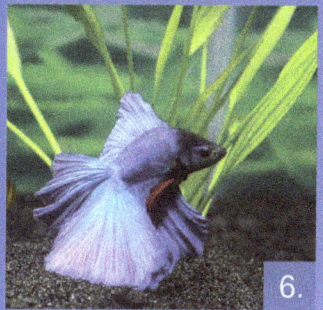

Can you match each of these common pets with its scientific name?   Turn the page to see the answers.

a. **Meriones unguiculatus**
/ mair-ee-**own**-es   uhn-gwee-**kyoo**-lah-tus /

b. **Felis catus**
/ **fee**-lis   **kah**-tuhs /

c. **Betta splendens**
/ **bay**-tuh   **splen**-dens /

d. **Coenobita clypeatus**
/ seen-oh-**bit**-uh   **cly**-pe-ait-us /

e. **Cavia porcellus**
/ **cave**-ee-uh   pore-**sel**-uhs /

f. **Canis lupus familiaris**
/ **kane**-is   **loo**-puhs   fah-mil-ee-**air**-is /

Answers from page 39

Answers from page 39

1 (f)

dog
*Canis lupis
familiaris*

2 (d)

hermit crab
*Coenobita
clypeatus*

3 (a)

gerbil
*Meriones
unguiculatus*

4 (e)

guinea pig
Cavia porcellus

5 (b)

cat
Felis catus

6 (c)

Betta
Betta splendens

Top Tips for Choosing a Pet

Adding a pet to your family is an important decision. It means taking responsibility for the pet's health and well-being and making a promise to care for the pet for the rest of its life.

Are you looking for an active pet or one that's easy to take care of? Do you want a pet that you can snuggle? Or are you interested in an unusual or exotic pet?

Think about:

1. Is the pet available for adoption from a shelter? There's a rescue or adoption organization for just about every type of pet.

2. How much time will it take to care for the pet?

3. Can you give the pet the attention and care that it will need?

4. Who will care for the pet when you're away from home?

5. How big will the pet get?

6. Can you provide the space and type of housing the pet needs?

7. Is this a safe pet for you and your family?

8. Can you afford the cost of the pet and its care?

9. Can you keep the pet where you live? Are there laws or housing rules to consider?

10. Do you already have a pet? If so, how will your current pet accept the new pet?

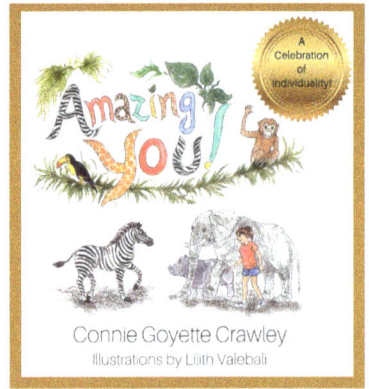

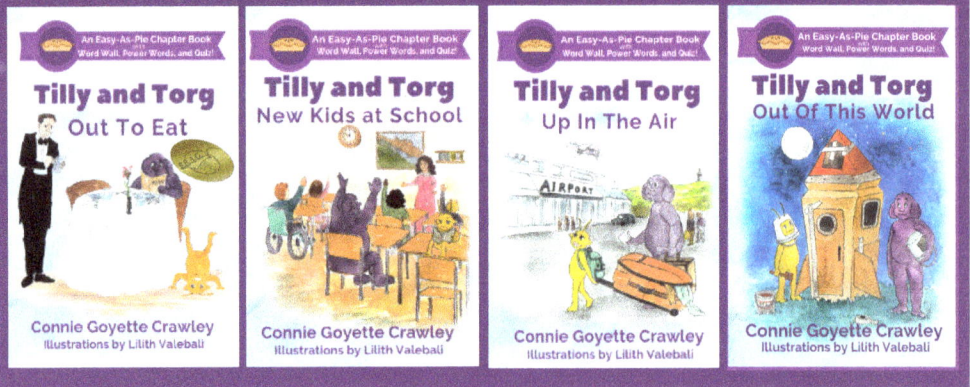

Connie Crawley is a former elementary school teacher,
a consultant for an educational software company,
and an award-winning author.

Jack is a German Shepherd mix,
a self-appointed "greeter" at the dog park,
and a relentless chipmunk chaser.

The Crawley family is grateful to
TenderHeart & Great Pyr Rescue
for their dedication to saving a life - one paw at at time!
Visit them at
http://tenderheartrescue.webs.com
or on Facebook

Find out more at conniecrawley.com

Copyright

Research Questions

Look back through the book to find the answers to these questions:

1. A group of frogs is called an _____ of frogs.

2. Canis lupus familiaris is the scientific name for a _____.

3. Ball pythons are native to _____.

4. What are three ways that an octopus can protect itself?

5. Emus are native to _____. The _____, which lives in _____ is closely related to the emu.

6. The longest type of stick insect ever found is the *Phryganistria chiesis Zhao*. It is over _____ inches long.

7. _____ and _____ can protect themselves by releasing a bad smell.

8. Bearded dragons are also known as _____.

9. _____ are closely related to anteaters. They are also called _____.

10. How long can capybaras stay under water?

If you could adopt any pet, what would you choose?   Why?

www.ingramcontent.com/pod-product-compliance
Lightning Source LLC
Chambersburg PA
CBHW041218030426

42336CB00023B/3385

9 780999 866147 6